I0702080

Table Of Contents

Chapter 1: Introduction to Indoor Plants and Decor Styles

Understanding the Impact of Indoor Plants on Home Decor

In the realm of interior design, indoor plants have emerged as a powerful tool that not only adds a touch of nature to your living spaces but also enhances the overall ambiance and aesthetic appeal of your home. For plant lovers, incorporating indoor plants into specific decor styles like bohemian or minimalist can transform any ordinary space into a breathtaking oasis. In this subchapter, we will explore the profound impact of indoor plants on home decor, with a focus on creating a boho atmosphere.

The bohemian decor style embraces a carefree, eclectic, and nature-inspired vibe. It is all about blending various textures, colors, and patterns to create a warm and inviting space. Indoor plants perfectly complement this style by bringing a sense of life and vitality to every corner of your home. The lush green foliage, combined with trailing vines and vibrant flowers, creates an enchanting visual display that exudes a bohemian atmosphere.

Not only do indoor plants contribute to the visual appeal, but they also have a positive impact on your well-being. Numerous studies have shown that plants improve air quality by removing toxins and releasing oxygen, creating a healthier indoor environment. The presence of plants also reduces stress and anxiety, promoting a sense of calmness and tranquility.

When it comes to minimalist decor, which focuses on simplicity and clean lines, indoor plants play a crucial role in adding a touch of nature without overwhelming the space. The elegance of indoor plants lies in their ability to create a harmonious balance between the natural world and minimalist design principles. By carefully selecting a few well-placed plants with sculptural shapes and lush green leaves, you can achieve a minimalistic look that is both refreshing and visually appealing.

Indoor plants offer endless possibilities for incorporating them into your home decor. From hanging plants cascading from macrame planters to large potted plants placed strategically in corners, the options are vast. Additionally, don't overlook the impact of planters and pots themselves. Choosing unique and decorative planters can further enhance the overall boho or minimalist aesthetic.

In conclusion, indoor plants have a profound impact on home decor, especially when it comes to specific styles like bohemian or minimalist. Whether you desire a boho oasis or a minimalist haven, incorporating indoor plants will undoubtedly transform your space into a visually stunning and calming environment. So, unleash your creativity, experiment with different plant varieties and arrangements, and bring the jungle vibes into your home!

Exploring Different Decor Styles and Their Influence on Indoor Plant Selection

When it comes to creating a beautiful and harmonious indoor space, the choice of decor style plays a crucial role. Each decor style has its unique characteristics, and selecting the right indoor plants can greatly enhance the overall aesthetic. In this subchapter, we will delve into the different decor styles and how they influence the selection of indoor plants, with a specific focus on bohemian and minimalist styles.

Bohemian Style:
Bohemian decor is all about creating a relaxed and eclectic atmosphere. This style embraces an abundance of colors, patterns, and textures. When selecting indoor plants for a bohemian space, aim for a mix of lush, cascading foliage and bold, vibrant blooms. Think hanging plants, such as pothos or string of pearls, to create a whimsical and free-spirited look. Succulents and cacti can also be incorporated, as their unique shapes and textures add to the boho vibe.

Don't be afraid to mix and match different plant varieties and showcase them in macrame hangers or vintage-inspired pots to truly capture the bohemian essence.

Minimalist Style:

Minimalism is characterized by simplicity, clean lines, and a minimalist color palette. The focus here is on creating a clutter-free and calming environment. When it comes to indoor plants for a minimalist decor style, less is more. Opt for plants with sleek and architectural shapes, such as snake plants or fiddle leaf figs. These plants not only add a touch of greenery but also serve as statement pieces. Potted ferns or monstera deliciosa can also be used to add a touch of nature without overwhelming the space. Keep the plant selection minimal and ensure they are placed strategically to create a sense of balance and tranquility.

Regardless of the decor style you choose, it is important to consider the lighting conditions and maintenance requirements of the indoor plants. Some plants thrive in bright, indirect light, while others can handle lower light conditions. Additionally, consider the level of care and attention you are willing to provide. Some plants require regular watering and misting, while others are more self-sufficient.

By understanding the influence of different decor styles on indoor plant selection, you can curate a space that reflects your personal style and brings nature indoors. Whether you lean towards the bohemian or minimalist aesthetic, there are countless plant varieties to choose from that will perfectly complement your decor and create a tranquil oasis within your home.

Chapter 2: The Bohemian Decor Style

Characteristics and Elements of Bohemian Decor

Bohemian decor, also known as boho style, is a vibrant and eclectic design aesthetic that celebrates free-spiritedness and creativity. It is a perfect style choice for plant lovers seeking to create a cozy oasis filled with indoor plants. The combination of lush greenery and bohemian elements can transform any space into a tranquil haven with a touch of whimsy. In this subchapter, we will explore the key characteristics and elements that define bohemian decor and how to incorporate them into your indoor plant-filled sanctuary.

One of the fundamental characteristics of bohemian decor is its embrace of natural materials and textures. This style often features elements like rattan, jute, macrame, and rustic wood. Integrate these materials into your plant display by incorporating macrame plant hangers, woven baskets for pots, or wooden shelves to showcase your indoor jungle. These natural elements will add warmth and depth to your bohemian oasis.

Another essential aspect of bohemian decor is the abundance of colors and patterns. Boho style is known for its vibrant color palette, with rich jewel tones, earthy hues, and pops of bold colors. When choosing plants for your bohemian oasis, opt for varieties with colorful foliage, such as the vibrant leaves of the croton or the rich purple of the tradescantia zebrina. Pair these plants with patterned textiles like Moroccan rugs, floral tapestries, or embroidered cushions to create a visually captivating space.

Bohemian decor is all about embracing a relaxed and informal atmosphere, with a mix of vintage and globally inspired pieces. Incorporate unique and one-of-a-kind finds into your plant-filled space, such as antique vases, vintage planters, or quirky trinkets collected during your travels. These elements add personality and a sense of wanderlust to your boho oasis.

Lastly, don't be afraid to embrace an abundance of indoor plants in your bohemian decor. Pile on the greenery, mix different sizes and shapes of plants, and create layers of foliage. Hanging plants, cascading vines, and tall potted plants all contribute to the lush and wild aesthetic of boho style.

In conclusion, bohemian decor is a perfect match for plant lovers looking to create a serene and vibrant indoor jungle. By incorporating natural materials, vibrant colors, unique vintage finds, and an abundance of indoor plants, you can transform your space into a boho oasis that exudes creativity and free-spiritedness. Let your plant collection thrive in this eclectic and whimsical style, and enjoy the jungle vibes of your bohemian sanctuary.

Choosing Indoor Plants for a Boho Vibe

If you are a plant lover and have a special affinity for the bohemian style, then you are in for a treat! Creating a boho oasis with indoor plants is not only a delightful endeavor but also a great way to infuse your space with a relaxed and free-spirited ambiance. The key lies in selecting the right plants that perfectly complement the boho vibe you wish to achieve.

When it comes to choosing indoor plants for a boho vibe, it's all about embracing lushness, vibrancy, and a touch of wildness. Here are a few plant suggestions that will help you achieve that desired bohemian aesthetic:

1. Pothos: This trailing vine with heart-shaped leaves is a classic choice for boho enthusiasts. Its cascading foliage adds a touch of wilderness to any space. Hang it in macrame plant hangers or let it trail down from a shelf to create a boho oasis.

2. Monstera: With its iconic split leaves, the Monstera plant is a must-have for any bohemian interior. Its large, tropical leaves instantly infuse a space with a sense of exoticism and adventure.

3. Snake Plant: The snake plant, with its upright, sword-like leaves, brings a touch of drama to any boho decor. It thrives in low light conditions and requires minimal care, making it a perfect choice for beginners.

4. Spider Plant: Known for its arching leaves adorned with tiny plantlets, the spider plant is a versatile choice for bohemian interiors.

Hang it from the ceiling, place it on a bookshelf, or let it cascade down from a planter to create a whimsical boho vibe.

5. Fiddle Leaf Fig: With its large, glossy leaves, the fiddle leaf fig is a statement-making plant that adds a touch of elegance to bohemian spaces. Place it in a woven basket or a vintage ceramic pot to enhance its boho charm.

6. Peace Lily: The peace lily's lush, dark green foliage and elegant white flowers bring a sense of tranquility to any boho oasis. It thrives in low light conditions, making it ideal for creating a cozy bohemian corner.

Remember, the key to achieving a boho vibe with indoor plants is to let your creativity flow. Mix and match different plant varieties, experiment with unique planters, and incorporate elements like macrame hangers, rattan baskets, and woven rugs to elevate the bohemian aesthetic of your space.

By carefully selecting and arranging indoor plants that embody the boho spirit, you can transform your home into a lush oasis that radiates a relaxed and free-spirited vibe. So, embrace the bohemian style, let your plants flourish, and enjoy the enchanting jungle vibes that come with it!

Creating a Bohemian Oasis with Indoor Plants

If you're a plant lover who is captivated by the enchanting bohemian decor style, you're in for a treat! In this subchapter, we will explore how indoor plants can transform your living space into a vibrant boho oasis. With their natural beauty and lushness, plants have the power to breathe life into any room, and when combined with bohemian elements, they can create a truly magical atmosphere.

The bohemian decor style is characterized by its eclectic and free-spirited nature. It embraces a mix of colors, patterns, and textures, creating a warm and inviting ambiance. Indoor plants perfectly complement this aesthetic, adding an organic touch to the overall design. To create your own bohemian oasis, consider the following tips:

1. Embrace Variety: The bohemian style celebrates diversity and embraces a mix of different plant species. Incorporate a variety of sizes, shapes, and leaf colors to add visual interest to your space. Think about incorporating trailing plants like Devil's Ivy or colorful foliage plants like Calathea to create a lush and dynamic display.

2. Macrame Hangers and Plant Stands: Macrame hangers and plant stands are iconic bohemian decor elements. They not only elevate your plants to eye-catching levels but also add a touch of vintage charm to your space. Hang your plants near windows or in corners, or use plant stands to create layered displays.

3. Play with Textiles: Bohemian decor is all about layering textures. Add woven baskets, tapestries, or colorful rugs beneath your plant displays to create a cozy and inviting atmosphere. These textiles will accentuate the natural beauty of your indoor plants and add depth to your overall boho oasis.

4. Create a Plant Corner: Dedicate a specific area in your home as a plant corner. Arrange plants of varying heights and sizes on shelves or a plant ladder to create a visually appealing and lush display. Incorporate other bohemian elements like dreamcatchers or vintage artwork to enhance the overall boho vibe.

5. Low-Maintenance Plants: To maintain the laid-back and free-spirited nature of bohemian decor, opt for low-maintenance plants that don't require constant attention. Succulents, snake plants, and ZZ plants are perfect choices that thrive in various light conditions and are forgiving when it comes to watering.

By following these tips, you can transform your living space into a bohemian oasis filled with the beauty and vitality of indoor plants. Embrace the freedom and creativity of the boho style, and let your imagination run wild as you create a unique and enchanting sanctuary. Let your indoor plants be the stars of your bohemian decor, bringing nature's harmony and tranquility into your home.

Chapter 3: The Minimalist Decor Style

Principles and Features of Minimalist Decor

Minimalism has gained immense popularity in the world of interior design, and it has now extended its reach to the realm of indoor plants. Combining the beauty of nature with the simplicity of minimalist decor, plant lovers can now create stunning spaces that exude a sense of calm and tranquility. In this subchapter, we will explore the principles and features of minimalist decor that can be incorporated into your bohemian oasis with indoor plants.

At its core, minimalism advocates for a clutter-free, clean, and simplified environment. Embracing this concept with indoor plants allows you to create a harmonious balance between nature and design. The first principle of minimalist decor is to choose a limited color palette. Opt for neutral tones like whites, grays, and earthy tones for your walls and furniture, allowing the vibrant green hues of your indoor plants to take center stage.

Another important aspect of minimalist decor is to focus on functionality and purpose. Select indoor plants that not only add beauty to your space but also serve a purpose. For example, choose air-purifying plants like snake plants or peace lilies to enhance the air quality in your boho oasis.

Simplicity is key when it comes to minimalist decor. Avoid overcrowding your space with too many plants or accessories. Instead, opt for a few statement plants strategically placed around the room. This will create a visually appealing and uncluttered environment, allowing each plant to shine in its own right.

Incorporating natural materials is another feature of minimalist decor. Choose planters and pots made from materials like terracotta or wood to add warmth and texture to your space. Additionally, consider using natural fibers like jute or rattan for your plant hangers or decorative baskets.

Finally, lighting plays a crucial role in minimalist decor. Embrace natural light as much as possible by placing your indoor plants near windows or incorporating skylights. If natural light is limited, choose warm, soft lighting options that create a cozy and inviting atmosphere.

By incorporating these principles and features of minimalist decor into your bohemian oasis with indoor plants, you can create a space that is both visually stunning and calming. Remember, less is more when it comes to minimalist decor, allowing your indoor plants to take center stage and bring the beauty of nature into your home.

Selecting Indoor Plants for a Minimalist Aesthetic

Minimalism is a design style that focuses on simplicity, clean lines, and a clutter-free environment. If you are a plant lover looking to create a minimalist aesthetic in your home, selecting the right indoor plants is crucial. These plants should complement your minimalist decor while adding a touch of greenery and tranquility to your space. In this subchapter, we will explore the best indoor plants for a minimalist aesthetic and how to care for them.

When it comes to selecting indoor plants for a minimalist aesthetic, less is more. Choose plants with simple, geometric shapes and clean foliage. Some popular choices include snake plants, peace lilies, and philodendrons. These plants have sleek leaves and can thrive in low-light conditions, making them perfect for minimalist spaces.

Another important aspect of a minimalist aesthetic is a neutral color palette. Opt for plants with green foliage rather than vibrant flowers. Plants like ZZ plants, pothos, and monstera deliciosa are excellent choices as they offer lush foliage without overwhelming your space.

In addition to selecting the right plants, it is essential to consider the pots or planters. For a minimalist look, choose pots in neutral colors such as white, black, or gray. Ceramic or concrete pots with clean lines and simple shapes work well with a minimalist aesthetic.

When it comes to caring for your indoor plants, minimalist or not, it's crucial to understand their specific needs. Most indoor plants thrive in well-draining soil and require water only when the top inch of soil is dry. Overwatering can be detrimental to the health of your plants and can disrupt the minimalist aesthetic by causing unsightly mold or mildew.

Regularly dust your plant's leaves to keep them clean and vibrant. This not only improves their appearance but also ensures optimal photosynthesis. Additionally, consider rotating your plants every few weeks to ensure even growth and prevent them from leaning towards the light source.

Remember, creating a minimalist aesthetic with indoor plants is all about simplicity and balance. Choose a few statement plants that fit your space and care for them properly. By selecting the right plants, placing them in minimalist pots, and giving them proper care, you can achieve a stunning and serene ambiance in your minimalist oasis.

In conclusion, selecting indoor plants for a minimalist aesthetic requires careful consideration. Opt for plants with simple foliage, geometric shapes, and a neutral color palette. Choose pots or planters that align with your minimalist style, and ensure you provide proper care to maintain their health and appearance. With these tips, you can create a harmonious and serene space that combines the beauty of indoor plants with the simplicity of minimalism.

Incorporating Indoor Plants into Minimalist Spaces

Minimalist interior design has gained immense popularity in recent years for its clean lines, simplicity, and clutter-free aesthetic. While minimalist spaces are often associated with a lack of decoration, incorporating indoor plants can add a touch of warmth and life to these serene environments. In this subchapter, we will explore how to seamlessly integrate indoor plants into minimalist spaces, creating a harmonious balance between simplicity and nature.

One of the key principles of minimalism is to focus on few but well-chosen items. When selecting indoor plants for a minimalist space, opt for plants with clean lines and uncomplicated shapes. Succulents and cacti are excellent choices as they possess minimalist qualities in their architectural forms. Their sculptural shapes and geometric patterns effortlessly blend with the simplicity of minimalist décor.

Another important aspect to consider is the color palette. Minimalist spaces typically feature a neutral color scheme with shades of white, gray, and beige. Indoor plants can introduce a pop of vibrant green, serving as a focal point in an otherwise monochromatic setting. Think about incorporating plants with large, glossy leaves such as the fiddle-leaf fig or the snake plant, as their lush foliage can create a stunning contrast against a minimalist backdrop.

To maintain the clean and uncluttered look of minimalist spaces, opt for sleek and minimalistic planters. Choose planters in neutral colors or materials like ceramic, concrete, or metal. These minimalist planters will seamlessly blend with the overall aesthetic, allowing the plants to take center stage without overpowering the space.

When arranging indoor plants in a minimalist space, less is more. Instead of overcrowding the area with numerous plants, select a few statement pieces strategically placed throughout the room. A single large plant in a corner or a small grouping of plants on a side table can have a powerful impact in a minimalist space.

Incorporating indoor plants into minimalist spaces can create a calming and inviting atmosphere. The presence of nature indoors not only adds visual interest but also improves air quality and promotes a sense of well-being. By following the principles of minimalism and carefully selecting plants and planters, you can effortlessly infuse your minimalist space with the beauty of nature. Embrace the harmony between simplicity and greenery, and watch as your minimalist oasis blossoms into a serene and vibrant haven.

Chapter 4: Building Your Indoor Plant Collection

Understanding the Needs of Indoor Plants

To create the perfect boho oasis with indoor plants, it is crucial to understand the specific needs of these green beauties. Indoor plants have unique requirements that differ from their outdoor counterparts, and by catering to these needs, you can ensure their optimal growth and health. Whether you are a devoted plant lover or someone seeking to enhance their bohemian or minimalist decor style, understanding the needs of indoor plants is the first step towards creating a thriving indoor jungle.

Lighting plays a vital role in the life of indoor plants. While some plants thrive in bright, direct sunlight, others prefer indirect or filtered light. As a plant lover, it is essential to identify the lighting requirements of each plant species and place them accordingly. For bohemian decor, consider hanging plants near windows or using macramé plant hangers to create a whimsical effect. For minimalist decor, choose plants that can thrive in low-light conditions and place them strategically to add a touch of green without overwhelming the simplicity of the space.

Watering is another crucial aspect of caring for indoor plants. Overwatering or underwatering can be detrimental to their health. Different plant species have different watering needs, and it is essential to research and understand the specific requirements of each plant. Bohemian decor enthusiasts may opt for plants that thrive in humid environments, such as ferns or tropical plants, while minimalist decor lovers may prefer succulents that require less frequent watering.

Humidity levels also play a significant role in maintaining healthy indoor plants. Some plants thrive in high humidity, while others prefer drier conditions. Consider using a humidifier or placing plants in bathrooms or kitchens with higher moisture levels for bohemian decor. Minimalist decor lovers may choose plants that can tolerate lower humidity levels, such as snake plants or ZZ plants.

In addition to lighting, watering, and humidity, it is crucial to provide the right kind of soil, proper drainage, and occasional fertilization to indoor plants. By understanding these needs and catering to them, you can create a boho oasis with indoor plants that perfectly complements your decor style.

Remember, each plant has its own unique requirements, so it is essential to research and understand the specific needs of the plants you choose. By providing the right conditions, you can create a thriving indoor jungle that brings life, beauty, and a touch of boho or minimalist elegance to your space.

Essential Indoor Plant Species for Different Decor Styles

When it comes to creating a thriving and visually appealing indoor jungle, choosing the right plants for your specific decor style is crucial. Whether you are a bohemian enthusiast or a minimalist lover, there are indoor plant species that can perfectly complement and enhance your chosen aesthetic. In this subchapter, we will explore the essential indoor plant species for different decor styles, helping plant lovers create their own oasis.

1. Bohemian Decor Style:
Bohemian decor is all about embracing a carefree and eclectic vibe. To achieve this look, consider incorporating plants with lush foliage and vibrant colors. Some essential indoor plant species for bohemian style include Monstera deliciosa, commonly known as the Swiss Cheese Plant, with its large, unique leaves, and Calathea varieties such as Calathea orbifolia or Calathea medallion, which display intricate patterns on their foliage. Other great options include the Spider Plant (Chlorophytum comosum) and the Peace Lily (Spathiphyllum), both of which add a touch of elegance to any boho-inspired space.

2. Minimalist Decor Style:
Minimalist decor focuses on simplicity and clean lines. When it comes to indoor plants for this style, less is more. Choose plants that have a sleek and minimalist aesthetic, such as the Snake Plant (Sansevieria), with its tall, upright leaves, or the ZZ Plant (Zamioculcas zamiifolia), which features glossy, dark green foliage. Another excellent choice is the Fiddle Leaf Fig (Ficus lyrata), with its large, broad leaves that add a statement to any minimalist room. These plants not only provide a touch of nature but also create a sense of calm and tranquility.

Remember, the key to incorporating plants into your decor style is to consider their form, color, and overall aesthetic. Whether you are going for a bohemian or minimalist look, these essential indoor plant species will help you create a harmonious and visually stunning indoor jungle.

In conclusion, Jungle Vibes: Creating a Boho Oasis with Indoor Plants provides plant lovers with valuable insights into selecting the perfect indoor plant species for specific decor styles. By understanding the unique characteristics and aesthetics of different plants, individuals can create their own oasis that perfectly complements their chosen decor style. So, whether you are a bohemian enthusiast or a minimalist lover, let your indoor plants bring life and beauty into your space.

Caring for Indoor Plants to Ensure Optimal Growth and Health

As plant lovers, we understand the joy and beauty that indoor plants bring to our homes. Whether you are a fan of the bohemian style or prefer a minimalist aesthetic, incorporating indoor plants into your decor can create a stunning oasis. However, to ensure that your plants thrive and remain healthy, it is crucial to provide them with the proper care and attention. In this subchapter, we will explore essential tips for caring for indoor plants to ensure optimal growth and health in various decor styles.

1. Light: Understanding the lighting requirements of your indoor plants is key. For bohemian-style enthusiasts, plants like succulents and cacti thrive in bright, indirect sunlight. On the other hand,

minimalist decor lovers can opt for low-light plants like snake plants and ZZ plants that can tolerate lower light conditions.

2. Watering: Proper watering techniques are essential for maintaining healthy indoor plants. Overwatering can lead to root rot, while underwatering can cause dehydration. Always check the moisture level of the soil before watering, and make sure to provide drainage to prevent waterlogging.

3. Humidity: Many indoor plants, especially tropical varieties, thrive in environments with higher humidity. For bohemian-style enthusiasts, misting your plants regularly or placing them near a humidifier can create a lush, tropical atmosphere. Minimalist decor lovers can use pebble trays filled with water to increase humidity levels around their plants.

4. Fertilizing: Indoor plants require regular feeding to provide them with essential nutrients. Choose a balanced, water-soluble fertilizer and follow the instructions for application. Bohemian-style enthusiasts can experiment with organic fertilizers like compost tea, while minimalist decor lovers can opt for slow-release granules for convenience.

5. Pruning and Propagation: Regularly pruning your indoor plants helps maintain their shape and encourages new growth. Bohemian-style enthusiasts can embrace the wild, unruly nature of their plants, while minimalist decor lovers can focus on minimalist, clean lines. Propagation allows you to expand your plant collection and share the love with fellow plant enthusiasts.

Remember, each plant is unique and may have specific care requirements. Research the needs of your chosen indoor plants to ensure you provide them with the best care possible. By following these tips and tailoring them to your specific decor style, you can create a boho oasis or minimalist haven filled with thriving, healthy indoor plants. Happy planting!

Chapter 5: Styling and Arranging Indoor Plants

Choosing the Right Containers and Planters

When it comes to creating a boho oasis with indoor plants, choosing the right containers and planters is just as important as selecting the perfect plants. These vessels not only serve as homes for your beloved green friends but also play a significant role in enhancing the overall aesthetic of your space. In this subchapter, we will delve into the world of containers and planters, exploring the various options available and offering tips to help you make the best choices for your specific decor style.

For bohemian enthusiasts, the key is to embrace creativity and individuality. Opt for containers with unique shapes, textures, and patterns. Hand-painted ceramic pots or macramé plant hangers are perfect boho additions, adding a touch of whimsy and a hint of nostalgia to your indoor jungle. Don't be afraid to mix and match different container styles to create a visually captivating display.

On the other hand, if you lean towards a minimalist decor style, simplicity and clean lines are the way to go. Choose planters with sleek designs, such as geometric shapes or matte finishes. White or neutral-colored pots provide a minimalist backdrop that allows the beauty of your plants to take center stage. Consider using minimalist hanging planters or wall-mounted plant holders to maximize space and create a sleek, clutter-free environment.

Regardless of your decor style, it's crucial to consider the practical aspects of container selection. Ensure that your chosen containers have proper drainage holes to prevent overwatering and root rot. Additionally, consider the size of the plant and its future growth when selecting a container. A pot that is too small may restrict the plant's growth, while one that is too large can lead to excessive moisture retention.

In the next subchapter, we will explore the best plant choices for creating a boho oasis or minimalist haven, ensuring that your indoor plants perfectly complement your chosen decor style. Stay tuned for an exciting journey into the world of plant selection and styling!

Creating Eye-catching Displays with Indoor Plants

Indoor plants have become an essential element in home decor, adding a touch of nature and serenity to any space. For plant lovers who are looking to embrace specific decor styles such as bohemian or minimalist, incorporating eye-catching displays with indoor plants is a fantastic way to elevate the ambiance of your living space. In this subchapter, we will explore various techniques and ideas to create stunning displays that perfectly complement your chosen decor style.

Remember, the container is an essential part of the overall aesthetic, but it should never overshadow the beauty of your plants. Whether you're a bohemian enthusiast or a minimalist devotee, the right containers and planters will harmonize with your decor style and accentuate the natural beauty of your indoor jungle.

1. Bohemian Vibes:
Bohemian decor is all about embracing a free-spirited, eclectic style. To create eye-catching displays, consider using hanging macramé planters to showcase trailing plants like Devil's Ivy or String of Pearls. You can also incorporate vintage-inspired terracotta pots with colorful patterns and textures. Mixing different heights and sizes of plants will add depth and visual interest to your display. Additionally, don't be afraid to experiment with unique plant stands made from natural materials like rattan or bamboo.

2. Minimalist Elegance:

Minimalist decor focuses on clean lines, simplicity, and a clutter-free environment. To achieve an eye-catching display, opt for sleek, modern planters in neutral colors like white or black. Use plants with interesting leaf shapes, such as the Fiddle-Leaf Fig or the Snake Plant, to create a striking contrast against the minimalist backdrop. Grouping smaller plants together on a floating shelf or a minimalist plant stand will create a visually pleasing arrangement. Remember to keep the number of plants minimal, allowing each one to shine individually.

3. Mixing and Matching:

For those who prefer a blend of bohemian and minimalist styles, you can create a stunning display by mixing and matching elements from both. Combine macramé hangers with sleek white planters or pair a minimalist stand with a vibrant terracotta pot. Experiment with different textures, colors, and heights to strike the perfect balance between the two aesthetics.

Remember, the key to creating eye-catching displays with indoor plants lies in the balance between plant selection, container choice, and arrangement. Consider the natural lighting in your space and the specific care requirements of each plant. Regularly rotate and prune your plants to maintain a healthy and visually appealing display. By incorporating these ideas into your decor, you can effortlessly transform your living space into a boho oasis that reflects your unique style and love for indoor plants.

Utilizing Different Plant Arrangement Techniques for Specific Decor Styles

When it comes to decorating our homes with indoor plants, we often look for ways to complement our existing decor styles. Whether you have a bohemian-inspired space or a minimalist haven, there are various plant arrangement techniques that can help create a harmonious and cohesive atmosphere. In this subchapter, we will explore how to utilize different plant arrangement techniques for specific decor styles, focusing on bohemian and minimalist aesthetics.

Bohemian decor is all about embracing an eclectic and free-spirited vibe. It combines vibrant colors, patterns, and textures to create a visually stimulating environment. To complement this style, consider using a mix of different plant varieties in various sizes and shapes. Opt for plants with lush foliage, such as monsteras, ferns, and palms, to add a tropical touch to your boho oasis. Create a layered effect by arranging plants at different heights, using hanging planters, shelves, and macrame hangers. Incorporate decorative pots with intricate patterns or vibrant colors to enhance the bohemian aesthetic.

For those who prefer a minimalist decor style, simplicity and clean lines are key. When incorporating indoor plants into a minimalist space, it's important to focus on the quality of each plant rather than quantity. Choose a few statement plants, such as a fiddle-leaf fig or a snake plant, and place them strategically in the room. Keep the plant arrangement minimal and avoid overcrowding. Use sleek and modern planters in neutral tones to maintain a clean and streamlined look. Consider incorporating wall-mounted planters or vertical gardens to maximize space while adding a touch of greenery to your minimalist oasis.

No matter your preferred decor style, it's essential to consider the lighting conditions in your space. Some plants thrive in bright, indirect light, while others prefer low-light conditions. Pay attention to the specific light requirements of each plant and place them accordingly. Additionally, consider the care needs of each plant to ensure they thrive in their designated spots.

In conclusion, incorporating indoor plants into specific decor styles can enhance the overall ambiance of your space. By utilizing different plant arrangement techniques, you can create a bohemian oasis filled with lush foliage and vibrant colors, or a minimalist haven with clean lines and a few statement plants. Remember to consider lighting conditions and care requirements to ensure your plants thrive in their designated spots. So, let your creativity flourish and bring the jungle vibes into your home, transforming it into a beautiful oasis that reflects your unique style.

Chapter 6: DIY Projects for Boho-Inspired Indoor Plant Decor

Crafting Macrame Hangers for Hanging Plants

Macrame hangers have become increasingly popular among plant lovers, especially those who are looking to add a touch of bohemian or minimalist style to their indoor plant collection. These intricate and beautiful hangers not only allow you to showcase your greenery in a unique way but also add a touch of elegance and warmth to any space. In this subchapter, we will explore the art of crafting macrame hangers specifically designed for hanging plants, allowing you to create your very own boho oasis with indoor plants.

To start your macrame hanger project, you will need some basic materials such as macrame cord, a wooden dowel or metal ring for hanging, scissors, and a plant pot. Macrame cord comes in various thicknesses and colors, so you can choose the one that suits your taste and complements your interior decor style.

The first step is to measure and cut the macrame cord to the desired length. You will need eight equal strands of cord, each double the length you want your hanger to be. Fold them in half and attach them to the dowel or ring using a lark's head knot. This will create the top loop of your hanger.

Next, you can start creating the macrame knots. There are various knots you can use, such as the square knot, half-square knot, or spiral knot. These knots will form the body of your hanger and provide support for the plant pot. You can experiment with different knotting patterns to achieve the desired look.

Once you have reached the desired length for your hanger, it's time to create a secure knot at the bottom to hold the plant pot. You can use a gathering knot, crown knot, or any other decorative knot of your choice. Make sure the knot is tight enough to hold the weight of the plant pot.

After finishing the knot, carefully place your plant pot into the hanger and adjust it to the desired height. Ensure that the macrame hanger is securely holding the pot in place.

With your macrame hanger complete, you can now hang it in your desired location, whether it be near a sunny window or as a centerpiece in your living room. The combination of the lush greenery and the intricate macrame design will surely create a stunning visual impact.

By mastering the art of crafting macrame hangers for hanging plants, you can bring a touch of bohemian or minimalist style to your indoor plant collection. Let your creativity flow and experiment with different knotting techniques and cord colors to create a unique and personalized macrame hanger that perfectly complements your interior decor style. So, grab your materials and get ready to transform your space into a jungle oasis filled with beautiful hanging plants.

Creating DIY Plant Stands and Shelves

If you're a plant lover with a penchant for bohemian or minimalist decor styles, then this subchapter is perfect for you. In "Jungle Vibes: Creating a Boho Oasis with Indoor Plants," we understand the importance of incorporating indoor plants into specific decor styles to elevate your living space. In this subchapter, we'll explore the exciting world of DIY plant stands and shelves, allowing you to showcase your beloved green friends in a way that perfectly complements your boho or minimalist aesthetic.

When it comes to indoor plants, presentation is everything. By creating your own plant stands and shelves, you can add a personal touch to your space while ensuring that your plants are displayed in the most visually appealing way. Whether you prefer the earthy, relaxed vibes of bohemian decor or the clean, understated elegance of minimalism, there are countless DIY options for you to explore.

For the boho enthusiasts, consider using macrame plant hangers to suspend your plants from the ceiling or walls. This whimsical and artistic approach adds a touch of bohemian charm to any room. Alternatively, repurpose vintage wooden crates or wicker baskets to create unique and rustic plant stands. These eclectic pieces will give your indoor jungle a boho twist that is sure to impress.

If you lean more towards a minimalist aesthetic, opt for clean lines and simple designs. Try creating sleek wooden shelves that are both functional and stylish. These minimalist plant shelves will seamlessly blend into your interior while allowing your plants to take center stage. Additionally, consider incorporating geometric shapes and metallic accents into your DIY plant stands for a modern and sophisticated look.

With DIY plant stands and shelves, the possibilities are endless. Not only will you have fun creating these pieces, but you'll also have the satisfaction of knowing that your indoor plants are beautifully showcased in a way that complements your unique decor style.

So, whether you're a bohemian spirit or a minimalist at heart, this subchapter will guide you through the process of creating DIY plant stands and shelves that will transform your space into a stunning boho oasis or a sleek minimalist haven. Let your creativity flourish as you embark on this exciting journey of merging indoor plants with specific decor styles.

Designing Terrariums and Mini Indoor Gardens

Terrariums and mini indoor gardens are a fantastic way to bring a touch of nature into your home, creating a boho oasis that perfectly complements your indoor decor. Whether you lean towards a bohemian or minimalist style, these living arrangements offer versatility and charm. In this subchapter, we will explore the art of designing terrariums and mini indoor gardens, providing you with inspiration and practical tips to create your very own indoor botanical haven.

Terrariums are self-contained ecosystems that require minimal maintenance and are perfect for those with a busy lifestyle. To design a terrarium with a bohemian flair, opt for an assortment of lush green plants with varying textures and sizes. Incorporate elements like driftwood, pebbles, and crystals to add a mystical touch. Choose a glass container that showcases the beauty of your mini garden while allowing ample light to penetrate.

For a minimalist aesthetic, keep the design simple and clean. Select a single plant as the focal point and place it in a sleek, geometric container. Surround it with carefully arranged stones or sand for a Zen-like atmosphere. The key is to create a sense of balance and harmony through minimalism.

When designing mini indoor gardens, consider the decor style you want to enhance. For a bohemian vibe, incorporate trailing plants like String of Pearls or English Ivy. Add colorful flowers like African Violets or orchids for a pop of vibrancy. Use macramé hangers or wooden shelves to display your mini garden, creating a whimsical and cozy atmosphere.

For a minimalist approach, opt for clean lines and simplicity. Choose plants with architectural shapes, such as Snake Plants or ZZ Plants. Place them in modern, ceramic pots with neutral colors. Group them together or create a mini bonsai garden for a captivating focal point.

Regardless of your decor style, ensure your terrarium or mini indoor garden receives adequate light. Most indoor plants thrive in bright, indirect light, but be cautious of direct sunlight as it may scorch delicate leaves. Regularly misting your mini garden will help maintain humidity levels and keep the plants healthy.

Designing terrariums and mini indoor gardens is an exciting opportunity to cultivate your creativity and showcase your unique style. Whether you prefer a bohemian oasis or a minimalist sanctuary, these living arrangements will add beauty and tranquility to your indoor space. So, grab your gardening tools and let your imagination run wild as you create your own lush paradise.

Chapter 7: Maintaining a Harmonious Indoor Plant Decor

Regular Plant Care and Maintenance Routines

In the pursuit of creating a boho oasis with indoor plants, it is important to establish regular plant care and maintenance routines. By giving your plants the attention they need, you can ensure they thrive and enhance the overall aesthetic of your space. In this subchapter, we will explore the essential tasks and practices that will keep your indoor plants healthy and vibrant.

Watering is a fundamental aspect of plant care. Different plants have varying water requirements, so it is crucial to research and understand the specific needs of each plant in your boho oasis. Overwatering can lead to root rot and other issues, while underwatering can cause wilting and stunted growth. Finding the right balance is key. Consider using a moisture meter to determine when it's time to water your plants, as it can provide accurate readings and prevent over or underwatering.

Alongside watering, providing adequate light is vital to ensure the vitality of your indoor plants. Most indoor plants thrive in bright, indirect light, but some may have specific light requirements. Consider the placement of your plants in relation to windows and adjust accordingly. Regularly rotating your plants can also prevent them from leaning towards the light source and promote even growth.

Plant nutrition is another crucial aspect of regular plant care. Applying a balanced fertilizer can provide the necessary nutrients to support healthy growth. However, it's essential to follow the instructions and avoid overfertilizing, as this can lead to burns and other complications. Organic fertilizers are often a great choice for plant lovers who prefer a more natural approach.

Dust can accumulate on plant leaves over time, hindering their ability to photosynthesize effectively. Regularly dusting your plants with a soft cloth or using a gentle spray of water can help keep their foliage clean and glossy. This not only enhances their appearance but also improves their overall health.

Monitoring for pests is also a vital part of plant care and maintenance. Common indoor plant pests include aphids, spider mites, and mealybugs. Regularly inspecting your plants for signs of infestation and taking proactive measures such as using natural pest control methods or isolating affected plants can prevent the spread of pests and protect the health of your indoor jungle.

By incorporating these regular plant care and maintenance routines into your boho oasis, you can create an environment where your indoor plants can flourish. Remember, each plant is unique, so take the time to research and understand the specific needs of your plant babies. With dedication and care, your indoor plants will not only beautify your space but also bring the jungle vibes you desire.

Troubleshooting Common Indoor Plant Issues

As plant lovers, we know that indoor plants can bring a touch of nature and beauty to any space, especially when it comes to creating a boho oasis or minimalist decor style. However, just like any living thing, indoor plants can sometimes experience issues that may hinder their growth or affect their overall health. In this subchapter, we will explore some of the most common indoor plant issues and provide you with practical troubleshooting tips to keep your green companions thriving.

One common problem many plant enthusiasts face is overwatering. While it's essential to provide your plants with the right amount of hydration, excessive watering can lead to root rot and other complications. To avoid this, always check the moisture levels of the soil before watering. Allow the top layer to dry out between waterings and adjust the frequency based on the specific needs of your plant.

On the other hand, underwatering is another issue that can hinder the growth of your indoor plants. Signs of underwatering include wilting, yellowing leaves, and dry soil. To address this problem, ensure you are providing adequate water to your plants. Consider using a moisture meter to accurately determine when your plants need watering and adjust accordingly.

Another common issue is inadequate lighting. Different plants have varying light requirements, and it's crucial to provide them with the right amount of light to thrive. If your plants are not receiving enough light, they may exhibit symptoms such as leggy growth or pale leaves. Consider moving them to a brighter spot or supplementing with artificial grow lights to ensure they get the proper amount of light they need.

Pests can also be a nuisance for indoor plants. Common pests include aphids, spider mites, and mealybugs. To combat these intruders, regularly inspect your plants for any signs of infestation. If you spot any pests, isolate the affected plant, and treat it with appropriate organic pest control methods or insecticidal soap.

Lastly, indoor plants can sometimes suffer from nutrient deficiencies. Signs of nutrient deficiencies include yellowing leaves, stunted growth, or overall poor health. To address this issue, consider using organic fertilizers specifically formulated for indoor plants. Follow the recommended dosage and frequency to ensure your plants receive the necessary nutrients to thrive.

By understanding and troubleshooting these common indoor plant issues, you can ensure that your indoor plants not only enhance your boho oasis or minimalist decor but also thrive in their environment.

Remember, a little care and attention can go a long way in keeping your green companions healthy and vibrant.

Refreshing and Updating Your Indoor Plant Decor Over Time

One of the most exciting aspects of having indoor plants is the opportunity to refresh and update your plant decor over time. As plant lovers, we understand the desire to constantly experiment and find new ways to showcase our beloved green companions. In this subchapter, we will explore how you can refresh and update your indoor plant decor to reflect your evolving style and keep your space looking vibrant and inviting.

Whether you have embraced the bohemian vibes or minimalist aesthetics, indoor plants have the incredible ability to complement any decor style. However, as trends change and personal preferences evolve, it's essential to adapt your plant decor accordingly. Here are some tips to help you refresh and update your indoor plant decor over time:

1. Assess your space: Begin by evaluating your current indoor plant setup. Consider the layout, the number of plants, and how they interact with other elements in the room. Take note of what you love about your current decor and identify areas where you feel it could use a refresh.

2. Experiment with plant placement: Plants can completely transform a room, so don't be afraid to experiment with different

plant placements. Move them around, group them together, or create a focal point with a statement plant. Changing the arrangement can breathe new life into your space and give it a fresh look.

3. Introduce new plant varieties: Expand your plant collection by introducing new plant varieties. Explore plants that complement your decor style, such as lush tropical plants for a bohemian vibe or sleek and sculptural plants for a minimalist setting. Adding new plants can add visual interest and create a dynamic atmosphere.

4. Incorporate decorative elements: Enhance your indoor plant decor with decorative elements that align with your chosen style. For bohemian enthusiasts, consider macrame plant hangers or woven baskets. Minimalists may opt for sleek plant stands or geometric planters. These accessories can instantly update your decor and add a personal touch.

5. Stay updated with trends: Keep an eye on the latest trends in indoor plant decor. This doesn't mean you have to follow every trend, but it can inspire you to try new ideas and incorporate fresh elements into your space. Stay connected with online communities, blogs, and magazines dedicated to indoor plants for inspiration.

In conclusion, refreshing and updating your indoor plant decor over time allows you to continuously evolve your space and infuse it with your personal style. By experimenting with plant placement, introducing new plant varieties, incorporating decorative elements, and staying updated with trends, you can create a boho oasis or minimalist haven that reflects your individual taste and keeps your indoor plant decor forever captivating. So, let your creativity flourish and embrace the joy of transforming your space with the power of indoor plants.

Chapter 8: Showcasing Your Boho Oasis

Capturing Instagram-Worthy Photos of Your Indoor Plant Decor

In today's digital age, capturing visually stunning photos of your indoor plant decor has become a popular trend among plant lovers. There's something magical about sharing the beauty of your indoor jungle with the world, and Instagram provides the perfect platform to showcase your green thumb skills. Whether you're a bohemian enthusiast or a minimalist at heart, this subchapter will guide you on how to capture those perfect Instagram-worthy shots of your indoor plant decor.

1. Find the Perfect Lighting: Lighting is crucial when it comes to photography, and indoor plants are no exception. Natural light is the best choice for capturing the true colors and textures of your plants.

Position your plants near a window or in a well-lit area to ensure the best lighting conditions for your photos.

2. Set the Stage: Creating a visually appealing background is essential for indoor plant photography. Consider using a neutral-colored wall or a boho-inspired tapestry as a backdrop. Experiment with different textures and patterns that complement your decor style. This will add depth and interest to your photos, making them truly Instagram-worthy.

3. Play with Composition: Experiment with different angles and compositions to make your photos stand out. Try shooting from above to capture the symmetry of your plant collection or get down to their level for a more intimate perspective. Remember the rule of thirds, and place your focal point off-center for a visually pleasing composition.

4. Highlight Unique Details: Indoor plants have their own unique features, so be sure to highlight them in your photos. Capture the intricate patterns on the leaves, the delicate tendrils, or the vibrant flowers. Zoom in on these details to create captivating close-ups that will grab the attention of your audience.

5. Experiment with Props: Adding props to your indoor plant decor can take your photos to the next level. Consider incorporating elements like vintage books, macrame plant hangers, or artisanal pottery to enhance the overall aesthetic. Props can help tell a story and create a visually appealing composition.

6. Edit to Perfection: Post-processing is an essential part of creating Instagram-worthy photos. Experiment with filters and editing tools to enhance the colors, contrast, and sharpness of your images. However, remember to maintain a natural and authentic look to showcase the true beauty of your indoor plants.

By following these tips, you'll be well on your way to capturing stunning Instagram-worthy photos of your indoor plant decor. Remember, the key is to experiment, have fun, and let your creativity shine through. Happy snapping, plant lovers!

Sharing Your Indoor Plant Journey with the Plant Lover Community

One of the most rewarding aspects of being a plant lover is connecting with a community of like-minded individuals who share your passion for indoor plants. Whether you are a bohemian enthusiast or a minimalist at heart, there is a vibrant plant lover community waiting to welcome you with open arms. In this subchapter, we will explore the various ways you can share your indoor plant journey with this community and find inspiration from others who have similar decor styles.

Social media platforms like Instagram and Pinterest have become virtual hubs for plant lovers to showcase their indoor plant collections and exchange ideas. These platforms allow you to share your plant-filled spaces with the world, and in turn, gather inspiration from others who have embraced the bohemian or minimalist aesthetic. Use hashtags specific to your decor style, such as #bohoindoorplants or #minimalistgreenery, to connect with fellow plant enthusiasts and discover new ways to incorporate plants into your home.

Another way to share your indoor plant journey is by joining online forums and communities dedicated to indoor gardening and specific decor styles. These forums provide a space for plant lovers to ask questions, share tips, and seek advice from experienced enthusiasts. Engaging in conversations with others who have similar decor styles can lead to valuable insights and foster a sense of camaraderie within the community.

Consider attending plant swaps or plant meetups in your local area. These events bring together plant lovers of all decor styles, allowing you to network, exchange plants, and learn from others in person. You may even make lifelong friends who share your passion for indoor plants and specific decor styles.

If you are feeling particularly adventurous, you can start your own blog or YouTube channel to document your indoor plant journey. This allows you to share your experiences, tips, and discoveries with a wider audience. By providing valuable content tailored to specific decor styles, such as bohemian or minimalist, you can attract a niche audience of plant lovers who resonate with your aesthetic.

Remember, the plant lover community is incredibly diverse and welcoming. Embrace the opportunity to connect with others who share your love for indoor plants and specific decor styles. By sharing your journey and learning from others, you will continue to

grow as a plant lover and create a boho oasis or minimalist haven
that is uniquely yours.

Inspiring Others to Create Their Own Boho Oasis with Indoor Plants

Subchapter: Inspiring Others to Create Their Own Boho Oasis with
Indoor Plants

Welcome to the enchanting world of indoor plants and the bohemian
oasis they can help you create in your own living space. In this
subchapter, we will delve into the art of incorporating indoor plants
into your home decor, specifically focusing on the bohemian style.
Whether you are a seasoned plant lover or just starting your journey,
this chapter will inspire you to transform your space into a lush and
vibrant sanctuary.

The bohemian style is all about free-spiritedness, creativity, and a
connection to nature. It embraces a relaxed and eclectic ambiance,
combining various patterns, textures, and colors. Indoor plants play a
crucial role in achieving the boho aesthetic, as they bring life,
freshness, and a sense of tranquility to any room. So, let's explore
how you can infuse your space with jungle vibes and create your
own boho oasis.

First and foremost, consider the types of indoor plants that align with
the bohemian style. Think about lush foliage, hanging plants, trailing
vines, and cascading leaves. Some popular choices include pothos,
monstera, spider plants, and ferns. These plants not only add a touch

of greenery but also create a sense of depth and movement, embracing the boho philosophy of embracing imperfections and the beauty of wild, untamed nature.

To truly capture the bohemian spirit, focus on incorporating natural materials and textures into your plant displays. Opt for macrame plant hangers, woven baskets, or terracotta pots. These earthy elements perfectly complement the organic beauty of indoor plants and add a touch of rustic charm to your boho oasis.

Additionally, consider creating cozy nooks and relaxing corners where you can showcase your indoor plant collection. Think about adding floor pillows, vintage rugs, and dreamcatchers to enhance the boho vibe. By combining these elements with your green companions, you will create inviting spaces that encourage relaxation, creativity, and self-expression.

Remember, the bohemian style is all about personalization and embracing your unique taste. So, don't be afraid to experiment with different plant combinations, display techniques, and decorative accents. Let your creativity run wild and allow your indoor plants to be the focal point of your boho oasis.

In conclusion, indoor plants have the power to transform any space into a bohemian haven. By incorporating lush foliage, natural materials, and personal touches, you can create a vibrant and inspiring sanctuary that reflects your love for plants and the boho aesthetic. So, let your imagination roam free and embark on the journey of creating your own jungle vibes-filled boho oasis with indoor plants.

Chapter 9: Conclusion

Reflecting on the Journey of Creating a Boho Oasis with Indoor Plants

Welcome to the subchapter "Reflecting on the Journey of Creating a Boho Oasis with Indoor Plants" from our book, "Jungle Vibes: Creating a Boho Oasis with Indoor Plants." This subchapter is dedicated to all the plant lovers out there who are seeking to infuse their homes with the vibrant and eclectic bohemian style.

Creating a boho oasis with indoor plants is a journey filled with creativity, self-expression, and a deep connection with nature. It is about transforming your living space into a sanctuary that reflects your unique personality and love for greenery. As you embark on this journey, it is important to reflect and appreciate the transformative power that indoor plants can have on your home.

The bohemian style is known for its free-spirited, laid-back, and unconventional nature. It embraces a mix of patterns, textures, and colors, creating a visually stimulating environment. Indoor plants play a crucial role in achieving this aesthetic, as they bring life, warmth, and a sense of adventure into any space.

Reflecting on your journey of creating a boho oasis with indoor plants allows you to appreciate how your plant collection has evolved over time. Remember the excitement of discovering new plant species, the joy of nurturing them, and the satisfaction of seeing them thrive. Each plant has a story to tell, and they have become an integral part of your home's decor.

The beauty of incorporating indoor plants into a boho oasis lies in their versatility. From cascading vines to sculptural cacti and lush tropical foliage, each plant adds its own unique charm to your space. Reflect on how you have carefully curated a variety of plant species, considering their growth habits, lighting requirements, and compatibility with your decor style.

As you reflect on your journey, consider the impact that indoor plants have had on your overall well-being. The presence of greenery indoors promotes relaxation, reduces stress, and improves air quality. Take a moment to appreciate how your boho oasis with indoor plants has become a sanctuary where you can escape the chaos of the outside world and find solace in the beauty of nature.

In conclusion, creating a boho oasis with indoor plants is a transformative journey that allows you to infuse your living space with personal expression and a deep connection with nature. Reflect on how your plant collection has evolved, the stories each plant tells, and the impact they have had on your well-being. Embrace the beauty and versatility of indoor plants as you continue to create your own unique boho oasis. Let the jungle vibes inspire you on this incredible journey!

Embracing the Benefits and Joy of Indoor Plant Decor

Introduction:

Indoor plants not only bring a touch of nature into your home but also offer numerous benefits for your well-being. They have the power to transform any living space into a tranquil oasis, breathing life and personality into your home. This subchapter will explore the many benefits and joys of incorporating indoor plants into your home decor, with a particular focus on how they can enhance specific styles such as bohemian and minimalist.

Creating a Calming and Serene Environment:

Indoor plants have a remarkable ability to create a calming and serene atmosphere in any room. Their lush green foliage and gentle presence can help reduce stress, improve air quality, and promote a sense of tranquility. Whether you prefer a bohemian or minimalist decor style, indoor plants can be the perfect addition to create a soothing and inviting space.

Embracing Bohemian Vibes:

For those who resonate with the bohemian style, indoor plants can be a game-changer. Their wild and untamed nature perfectly complements the eclectic and free-spirited essence of boho decor. Whether you choose hanging plants, trailing vines, or large leafy specimens, indoor plants can add a touch of whimsy and natural beauty to your bohemian oasis.

Minimalism and Indoor Plants:

Contrary to popular belief, minimalist decor doesn't mean completely eliminating all elements of nature. In fact, indoor plants can seamlessly blend with minimalist aesthetics, adding life and warmth to clean lines and neutral colors. Opting for simple, low-maintenance plants like succulents or monstera can be an excellent way to embrace minimalism while still enjoying the benefits of indoor greenery.

The Joy of Indoor Gardening:

Indoor plant decor is not just about aesthetics; it also brings joy and a sense of fulfillment. Nurturing and watching your plants grow can be a therapeutic experience, providing a sense of accomplishment and connection with nature. Your indoor garden can become a source of inspiration and a sanctuary where you can unwind and find peace amidst the chaos of daily life.

Conclusion:

Embracing indoor plant decor is a delightful way to enhance your home's ambiance and infuse it with positive energy. Whether you're a plant lover with a bohemian soul or a minimalist seeking a touch of nature, indoor plants can effortlessly elevate your living space. So, dive into the world of indoor gardening, and let your home be transformed into a lush, green haven where beauty and tranquility coexist in perfect harmony.

Encouraging Continued Exploration and Experimentation with Indoor Plants in Different Decor Styles

One of the most exciting aspects of incorporating indoor plants into your home decor is the endless possibilities for creativity and personal expression. Whether you are a bohemian enthusiast or a minimalist aficionado, indoor plants can enhance and complement any decor style, allowing you to create a unique oasis that reflects your individual taste and personality.

For plant lovers who are drawn to the bohemian decor style, the key is to embrace the eclectic and free-spirited nature of this aesthetic. Think lush green foliage cascading from macrame hangers, vibrant and colorful pots, and a mix of textures and patterns in your plant displays. Experiment with a variety of plant species, such as the trailing Devil's Ivy or the bold and exotic Bird of Paradise, to add depth and visual interest to your boho oasis. Don't be afraid to play with unconventional plant arrangements, such as grouping plants of different heights and sizes or creating a living wall as a focal point. The bohemian decor style celebrates imperfections and the beauty of nature, so let your creativity run wild and create a space that feels organic and inviting.

On the other hand, if you are a fan of minimalism, you can still incorporate indoor plants into your decor in a way that maintains the clean and clutter-free aesthetic. Opt for sleek and simple planters in neutral tones, such as matte white or concrete, to create a sense of calm and tranquility. Choose plants with clean lines and minimalist shapes, like the popular Snake Plant or the elegant Peace Lily, to maintain a sense of simplicity. Grouping plants together in clusters or arranging them in a symmetrical pattern can create a visually pleasing and balanced display. Remember, less is more in minimalist decor, so choose a few carefully selected plants and allow them to shine in their simplicity.

No matter what your preferred decor style may be, the key to successfully incorporating indoor plants is to continue exploring and experimenting. Don't be afraid to step outside of your comfort zone and try new plant species, display techniques, and pot styles. Indoor plants are incredibly versatile and adaptable, making them the perfect companions for any decor style. So, let your imagination roam free, and create a boho oasis or minimalist haven that is uniquely yours, filled with the beauty and vibrancy of indoor plants.